put yourself together.
fix your crown.
-- adrian michael

TITLES YOU MIGHT LIKE
BY
ADRIAN MICHAEL

--

loamexpressions

blinking cursor

notes of a denver native son

blackmagic

lovehues

notes from a gentle man

blooming hearts

book of her book of she

Published by Creative Genius Publishing—
an imprint of lovasté | Denver, CO

To contact the author visit adrianmichaelgreen.com
Cover art provided by Shutterstock.com

ISBN-13: 978-1537267869
ISBN-10: 1537267868

Printed in the United States of America

;

book of her
book of she

they call her love
what a beautiful soul;
never done changing
she is ever evolving;
becoming her own
love song.
-- adrian michael

</> ;

her love can be cruel
but once inside
her love is naughty and nice
-- adrian michael

</> naughty and nice

you let go
she holds on
-- adrian michael

</> committed

her vibe is infectious.
-- adrian michael

</> her vibe is infectious

she wanted a better life
so she learned a new language
-- adrian michael

</> lifelong learner

do her no harm
& she will love you
for a lifetime.
-- adrian michael

</> good intentions

she treats you like her last breath
not expecting oxygen in return
-- adrian michael

</> breathless

her eyes —
landmarks in the constellation
legend of unsolved
mystery
-- adrian michael

</> legend

she will show you her heart
if you dare her not to
-- adrian michael

</> double dare

her love is sometimes funny
and sometimes serious;
it is never untrue
-- adrian michael

</> sometimes & never

10 things to love about her:
1-10 she loves herself
-- adrian michael

</> 10 things to love about her

they call her hurricane
because her temple is sweet
-- adrian michael

</> hurricane

she's not in a dark place
her heart just needs rest.
-- adrian michael

</> healing

she gets people drunk
for a living just by smiling
at those that pass her by.
-- adrian michael

</> 4o proof

she's ready for something real —
love, hope, trust...
she's ready for herself.
she's ready, she's ready.
-- adrian michael

</> ready

her indigo spirit was never meant
to be understood.
-- adrian michael

</> indigo

she is indigenous
to her own body.
-- adrian michael

</> native

wisdom advises her to forgive and
not forget how to love even if hurt.
-- adrian michael

</> wisdom

once she tried to outrun her light
then she embraced it and changed her life.
-- adrian michael

</> embrace

they tell her
she's not good enough
but dodging bullets
is one of her
super powers
-- adrian michael

</> bulletproof

she is beautiful ocean
her depth will take your breath away.
-- adrian michael

</> beautiful ocean

her heart aches for love —
she's not rushing into just anything.
-- adrian michael

</> patient

she has what she needs.
she is what she needs.
-- adrian michael

</> enough

she is her second chance at happiness.
-- adrian michael

</> second chance

full love.
that's what she deserves.
-- adrian michael

\</> full love

judge not her heart,
for you know not
what she's been through.
-- adrian michael

</> iceburg

and like the hands of a sculptor,
she took hold of her self and
reshaped an already beautiful soul.
-- adrian michael

</> sculptor

avoidance never served her.
she's learned that along the way.
-- adrian michael

</> lessons

she chooses herself.
she fights for herself.
she reclaims herself.
-- adrian michael

</> daily process

there's a thickness about her.
no matter how deep you go,
there's no limit to her depth.
-- adrian michael

</> no limit

she is unpredictable.
even she
surprises herself
with how incredible
she is.
-- adrian michael

</> unpredictable

give her touch so she can feel
the pulse of the relationship.
-- adrian michael

</> touch

one valiant thing she overcame
was letting go of her past
so she could thrive in her present.
-- adrian michael

</> release

treasure is anchored
underneath her soul.
she put it there.
hidden. for a true love
to find her.
-- adrian michael

</> hidden

she takes what matters.
she leaves what doesn't.
-- adrian michael

</> deliberate

her vibe is the prettiest.
-- adrian michael

</> pretty vibes

love the way she sins.
-- adrian michael

</> mint condition

let her be her true self.
be a mirror so you can be you, too.
-- adrian michael

</> mirror

she is a seed.
that must be nourished.
      lovingly. happily. presently.

she is a seed.
that waters herself.
slowly at first.
then all at once.
-- adrian michael

</> she is a seed

she gave herself the attention she deserved
from others. now they beg her to teach them
how to do the same.
-- adrian michael

</> teacher

she's an old soul
that believes in chivalry,
romance, and love.
-- adrian michael

</> old soul

a piece of her heart
is worth more than gold.
-- adrian michael

</> priceless

she eats better, sleeps better, thinks
better, loves better, feels better, lives
better, breathes better, is better.
-- adrian michael

</> self love

that's the thing about her heart,
she doesn't keep it to herself.
-- adrian michael

</> unconditional

she's the kind of magic
that you marry.
-- adrian michael

</> magic woman

when you see a queen, you'll know.
hearts bloom in her presence.
-- adrian michael

</> blooming hearts

she was always amazing.
sorry it took so long
to catch up to her universe.
-- adrian michael

</> slow burn

a true wanderer
is always home.
-- adrian michael

</> her

she's alive.
free. wild. centered.
beautiful.
-- adrian michael

</> she

a queen is a queen with or without
a queen, king, or crown.
-- adrian michael

</> queen

she left.
it was the only option she had.
-- adrian michael

</> departed

queen is a state of mind.
-- adrian michael

</> mindset

she's not ordinary, she's magic.
-- adrian michael

</> standard

speak her language.
she's fluent in yours.
-- adrian michael

</> learn

she is serious about who she shares
her space with. certain energies clash
with radiant light.
-- adrian michael

</> serious

treat her like
the goddess
that she is.
-- adrian michael

</> chivalry

when she lets you in
protect her heart.
-- adrian michael

\</> the golden rule

don't let her calm nature fool you.
she is militant and stands in her power.
-- adrian michael

</> powerful

she is the original
queen of hearts.
-- adrian michael

</> the original queen of hearts

you can't photoshop her heart.
-- adrian michael

</> no filter

she is known
for making fires
with her smile.
-- adrian michael

</> fire starter

wild is her profession.
-- adrian michael

</> professionally wild

she takes selfies so her soul
can see her self.
-- adrian michael

</> selfie queen

her fear isn't in getting hurt.
she is kevlar strong. be weary
of the one that breaks their teeth
trying to get to her heart.
-- adrian michael

</> kevlar strong

she lives in fire.
burning gives her comfort.
-- adrian michael

</> home

love is her wings.
she flutters effortlessly.
-- adrian michael

</> pretty wings

she is water.
powerful enough to drown you.
soft enough to cleanse you.
deep enough to save you.
-- adrian michael

</> she is water

the universe mixed her
with whiskey and honey
-- adrian michael

</> mixed

she is her own master, not looking for a
soulmate. she has herself. complete. whole.
she doesn't need what others offer. but if she
chooses you, beware. a heart like hers is a
polished diamond. make sure yours is
polished, too.
-- adrian michael

</> diamonds

her magic waters souls.
-- adrian michael

</> her magic waters souls

when she captures your heart
you'll never get it back.
-- adrian michael

</> command and conquer

sometimes her heart
scares her. and sometimes
it surprises her. how ever it
moves her. she listens.
she learns.
-- adrian michael

</> heart whisperer

she is sugar in a sour patch.
-- adrian michael

</> azúcar

the universe taught her how to be wild.
-- adrian michael

</> student

to some she is
offbeat. to her,
she is in tune
with her soul.
-- adrian michael

</> perception

what makes her beautiful is also
what condemns her. free spirits
will always be misunderstood.
-- adrian michael

</> free spirit

she is.
let her be.
like wine,
let her breathe.
-- adrian michael

</> she is wine

if it wasn't for her light
it would always be dark.
-- adrian michael

</> lüz

she is every little breath
and every little sigh.
the kind of wildflower
you look for but never pick.
she is the universe.
awe in human form.
-- adrian michael

</> soulmate

love is her compass. if it feels
right she goes in that direction.
-- adrian michael

</> compass rose

she
makes
breathing
look
beautiful.
-- adrian michael

</> art

even her shadow
is drenched in gypsy.
-- adrian michael

</> gypsy

do not remember her as she was. for
she will be different in a few hours.
think of her in waves: crashing onto
shore, murmuring back towards the
sun. when she returns she'll never be
the same. she is constantly evolving.
honor her as she is. look forward to
what she becomes. welcome her
newest version at dawn.
-- adrian michael

</> as she is

she grew so much.
no one recognized her.
but she did. her soul
had been waiting for
her to blossom.
-- adrian michael

</> in wait

she translates hearts.
-- adrian michael

</> translator

both lion and flower
require her water. may she
come to understand this.
-- adrian michael

</> nature

she made wings out of broken things
and rose above the ones that hurt her.
-- adrian michael

</> butterfly

love her like she's magic.
-- adrian michael

</> expectation

sometimes
she wants her heart
to be ravaged.
-- adrian michael

</> mrs. hyde

her faults are beauty marks.
-- adrian michael

</> perfection

she will love you best. let her.
-- adrian michael

</> allowance

love her demons
when they show up.
love her demons
when they go away.
-- adrian michael

</> pledge

she's a blessed herbal remedy.
healing souls one kiss at a time.
-- adrian michael

</> medicine woman

her skin has old marks from rustic daggers.
she is stronger now more than ever.
-- adrian michael

</> stronger

she has
nothing to hide.
she's just
waiting
for the one
who will cherish
her story.
-- adrian michael

</> herstory

there is room in her heart.
she just wants you to love her
with good intentions.
-- adrian michael

</> good intentions

no matter what she's beautiful.
-- adrian michael

</> no matter what she's beautiful

honor her universe.
-- adrian michael

</> honor her universe

she was tired of wading in
someone else's water. back
on dry land she danced
under the sun, melted,
and became her own ocean.
-- adrian michael

</> rain dance

each day she begins again.
creating her newest most beautiful version.
-- adrian michael

</> new beginnings

she has a southern heart
and a northern temper.
-- adrian michael

</> belle

water her and watch her bloom.
-- adrian michael

</> bloom

she took a breath so deeply
she found another galaxy
within her own body.
-- adrian michael

</> breathwork

love her beyond infinity. love her now.
passionately. extend the borders of your
being and impress upon her a love that
has no end, just limitless beginnings.
-- adrian michael

</> limitless

becoming magic is never easy
but she does it everyday when
she chooses to be herself.
-- adrian michael

</> becoming magic

she feels for the world
even when the world
may not feel for her.
-- adrian michael

</> citizen

she is the muse
that set the gods
on fire.
-- adrian michael

</> muse

sunflowers sprout from her soul.
-- adrian michael

</> sunflower

she's a new age soul that lives her truth,
cherishes relationships, loves abundantly,
respects her temple, handles her business,
speaks her mind, believes in herself, works
hard for what she wants, and is unapologetic
of the space she creates.
-- adrian michael

</> woman

she is brave.
she has to be. independence calls for it.
when her bravery is tested, she is bold.
she is strong. she is resilient. she is patient.
when she stands in her power, she is
unstoppable.
-- adrian michael

</> she is brave

she is subtle and strange in a beautiful way.
-- adrian michael

</> subtle and strange

the honey on her bones
blushes through her skin.
-- adrian michael

</> honey

she is the universal flower
that represents strength.
-- adrian michael

</> symbol

her love is the best damn love in the west.
-- adrian michael

</> which way is west?

she will always grow
wherever she's planted.
-- adrian michael

</> s.w.a.g

get to know her scars.
-- adrian michael

</> kin

she placed a billboard on her heart that
read, "love me gently, i'm still healing."
-- adrian michael

</> love her gently

same girl. different version.
-- adrian michael

</> revolution

she's not broken. she's millions
of puzzle pieces searching for the
meaning of each piece.
-- adrian michael

</> seeker

experience taught her.
hurt raised her.
neither defined her.
-- adrian michael

</> progression

show her why she chose you.
-- adrian michael

</> action

she has this way of knowing how you feel
before your feelings come up for air. maybe
it's the empath in her or the sorceress in her
soul.
-- adrian michael

</> heart reader

she's the color of love;
all shades of beautiful.
-- adrian michael

</> colorful

she closed her eyes
made a wish
and became her own
dream come true.
-- adrian michael

</> inhaler

she's a heart healer.
go to her. be healed.
-- adrian michael

</> heart healer

fly beside her.
don't cut her feathers
or roadblock her path.
-- adrian michael

</> partnership

she wakes up with freedom on her mind.
-- adrian michael

\</> freda

a good woman
is one of a kind.
look for her.
love on her.
-- adrian michael

</> a good woman

she's been hurt but she's still here.
she made jewelry out of her pain.
-- adrian michael

</> unbreakable

she was herself
long before
being herself
was vogue.
-- adrian michael

</> en vogue

she doesn't need you to save her,
she can save herself.
-- adrian michael

</> heroine

fall in love with her energy.
not her body.
-- adrian michael

</> priority

beautifully broken.
beautifully whole.
-- adrian michael

</> complex

she used to
    want your love;
    now, she just wants
    her own.
-- adrian michael

</> re-directed

the only lingerie she needs is the skin
that wraps around her bones.
-- adrian michael

</> negligee

deep and dope.
-- adrian michael

</> her, in three words

yeah, she's all that.
    and she's hers:
    her own blend of
    happy hour cocktails
    and bad ass songs
    that make her head nod
    to her own dope energy.
-- adrian michael

</> she's all that

she is a crystal.
her magic opens chakras
you didn't know you had.
-- adrian michael

</> pendulum

she's hard to get because
she's hard to get.
-- adrian michael

</> hard to get

her crazy sexy soul
is a diamond in the ocean.
find her.
-- adrian michael

</> crazy sexy soul

she is the fifth season.
-- adrian michael

</> love is coming

her bloom is different.
it carries no season nor
follows any pattern. she
becomes whatever she wants
when she wants. she is
as she should be —
beautiful and free.
-- adrian michael

</> her bloom is different

shallow she is not.
she is infinitely deep.
-- adrian michael

</> infinitely deep

being herself.
-- adrian michael

</> how she stays original

she rocks rompers with her hair
up or down. no makeup. she paints
the town with those who dare.
she is bad. she has always been bad.
-- adrian michael

</> she is bad

love is her first language.
-- adrian michael

</> fluent

she used to want your flowers.
now she grows her own.
-- adrian michael

</> florist

her sins make her more human.
-- adrian michael

</> sinner

she works out and eats healthy.
not for you. for her. she loves herself
enough to commit to such training.
she is disciplined. she is dedicated.
the type of woman you need in your life.
-- adrian michael

</> olympian

beautiful magic.
-- adrian michael

</> her, in two words

she is quite the raspy soul.
too wild to tame. too exquisite
to be ordinary.
-- adrian michael

</> too wild, too exquisite

she is bold. if that intimidates you,
get closer to her. let her teach you how to
respect her boldness.
-- adrian michael

</> bold woman

she is the most valuable plant.
water her.
-- adrian michael

</> gardener

she floats like a butterfly and stings like a
bee. her heart is kind but if you hurt her it
will be your end.
-- adrian michael

</> rumble

she is a knight polishing her armour.
carrying her own sword. fighting her
own battles. making her own glory.
-- adrian michael

</> knight

inhale her magic.
-- adrian michael

</> the big gulp

she's the kind of queen
that knows her crown
isn't on her head but
in her soul.
-- adrian michael

</> highness

she is a love practitioner.
her work is never done.
-- adrian michael

</> love doctor

she let go and found happiness.
-- adrian michael

</> alchemist

she is flawtiful.
all of her flaws
make her beautiful.
-- adrian michael

</> flawtiful

she is as soft as she looks
and as strong as she feels.
-- adrian michael

</> warrior

love her at her lowest.
that is when she needs
you most.
-- adrian michael

</> check in

she's in a serious relationship
with herself.
-- adrian michael

</> sel*fish*

she has everything she wants.
if you align with her, support
her dreams. she is down to
stand by yours, too.
-- adrian michael

</> commandment

she is a lover with attitude.
-- adrian michael

</> backbone

her voice
is all the poetry
you need.
-- adrian michael

\</> aria

she believed she could.
so she did. magic happened.
and she did it again.
-- adrian michael

</> faith

a gentle woman
opens her arms
to those who
need to be held.
-- adrian michael

</> gentle woman

queen on 'em.
-- adrian michael

</> lifestyle

heartbreak taught her that her kind of love
is not just for anybody. they have to be
ready and committed. they have to let go of
their past to be ready for their future. she
wants to give all of her love to one person
who will satisfy her soul in return. when she
opens her heart she gives all of her
in exchange for all of you.
-- adrian michael

</> the exchange

she wanders wherever her wild soul desires.
-- adrian michael

</> wild woman

her love is for real
so if you want magic
she has what you need.
-- adrian michael

</> dealer

she travels between time.
plotting to find new ways
to blend her imagination
with reality.
-- adrian michael

</> scientist

she misses the butterflies.
give them back to her.
-- adrian michael

</> catch and release

she is complicated and weird
and messy and nerdy and smart
and wonderful and misunderstood
and funny and carefree. as she
should be. she is as she is. she is
who she wants to be. and that is
a miracle. she is a miracle.
-- adrian michael

</> she is a miracle

she grew tired
of chasing storms
so she became one
and now
they chase after her.
-- adrian michael

</> storm

she has this rennaissance, bohemian,
chic, hipster, old soul, vintage, yogi,
classic, modern, authentic, beautiful
vibe going on.
-- adrian michael

</> she is all that + more

rooted to her ancestors
she knows who she is
who her people are
and where she is going.
she isn't just
standing on their shoulders
she is taking them with her.
-- adrian michael

</> roots

she will love you
from day one
to day infinity;
and that kind
of love is rare.
-- adrian michael

</> rare

you can't tame her soul.
-- adrian michael

</> soul centered

she is a queen.
her soul is royalty.
-- adrian michael

</> birthright

her love is under water.
you must practice the art
of holding your breath
without drowning.
-- adrian michael

</> underwater lover

she's a beautiful kind of wild.
-- adrian michael

</> queen

mind like hers.
heart like hers.
spirit like hers.
soul like hers.
no one compares
to her.
-- adrian michael

</> unparalled

queen. warrior. flower.
galaxy. empress. muse.
she is all things powerful
and beautiful and terrifying.
-- adrian michael

</> majesty

dear woman
;

dear woman,

thank you. you may rarely hear this. so
thank you. for being strong because you
are. for being soft because you are. for being
love because you are. i'm sorry for all the
times you have been taken advantage of and
overlooked. i'm sorry others made mistakes
and didn't know how to treat you. you are
a gift and you have always known this.
your big heart lets people in even if you risk
getting hurt. thank you for your bravery.
thank you for your courage. thank you for
your power. thank you for your beauty.

dear woman,

every battle you face is a victory because
you could choose to turn away but you are
not afraid to live. we have so much to learn
and love from you.

dear woman, we are because of you.
-- adrian michael

dear woman,

i do not know where you are on your
journey. you could be hurting, healing,
breaking, containing. you could be going
through something and feel like you are
all alone and no one understands the kind
of pain and anguish and emptiness inside.
you could be making one of the hardest
decisions in your life. you could be putting
back pieces of you and facing great difficulty
tracking down parts of you that you no
longer recognize. you could be at peace.
wherever you are, whoever you are with,
know that you are enough.

dear woman,

you deserve to be happy. whether you think
you are or are breaths away from being
happy, i encourage you to find it. keep it.
carry happiness with you. even when you
are up against heavy times that weigh you
down, let happiness be that crown that you
adorn yourself with. smile and grin wide
when you place that reminder on your
oh so beautiful skin, your dominion, your
body of great treasure, your beautiful world.

dear woman, you are such a gift.
-- adrian michael

dear woman,

i know that you feel trapped sometimes.
in too deep in relationship with someone
who you know doesn't treat you right. but
you have invested so much time and energy
that leaving them would make you feel
like some sort of failure. so you wait. you
wait until it gets better. and when they mess
up and remind you that you should have
left a long time ago, they do something nice
like apologize or buy you something or take
you to your favorite place. and you hold on
to that sliver of hope telling yourself that
they do love you. that they just don't always
know how to show it.

dear woman,

you are not a failure. your heart is in the
right place it's just in the wrong person.
please stop waiting for them to change or
you will continue to lose you. taking care
of their feelings should be suspended, now
begin to consider your own and move on.
true love is waiting for you in the form of
another lover, and in the form of your own.
depart and take a chance on discovering
the real love you have been kept from all
of this time.

dear woman, i see you. i honor you.
-- adrian michael

dear woman,

you have always been a queen. but
somewhere down the line you were told
otherwise. you were blindsided into thinking
that you must give away your power
and taking care of others was your only
responsibility. to deny your own wants and
wishes to elevate someone else even if it
meant turning down your voice. how cruel.
and the lie still exists in the form of gender
roles masked as tradition and you wore it
for so long that you became what they
wanted you to but in the core of your being
you felt like your life was meant to be more.

dear woman,

you were meant to be more. you are more.
if your mind intimidates, so what. if your
goals surprise, so what. your passion, your
dreams, your destiny, your heart, is in your
hands. never let someone dim your light so
that they may shine brighter. shine, queen.
illuminate every path you walk, every door
you open, every soul you touch. reclaim the
legend that was stolen from you and rewrite
the story of how queens came to glory.

dear woman, dear queen, i love you.
-- adrian michael

dear woman,

you are other worldly. the various
dimensions of you never end because even
at the bottom of your well you somehow
flex your magic and create other wells that
serve as extensions of womanhood; you are
what dreamers dream, exceedingly special.
you are beyond description. you are every
word and its synonym sibling. you are words
that haven't even been discovered yet. you
are generations of a collective, women
sewn into the fabric of your bones. you are
limitless. you are the milk of life. you are
honey. you are the entire ocean in just one
drop. you, magnificent breath, are becoming.

dear woman,

you are a wild wonder
who doesn't fit into a box.
remember to reign true
remember to love you
remember to be you
remember to love others.
remember,
even if broken
you are beautifully arranged;
putting back the pieces
makes you stronger my love;
your song isn't over
it has only just begun.
lovasté.
-- adrian michael

;

book of her
book of she

AZMA

stories. poems. quotes.

BY ADRIAN MICHAEL
COMING SOON

Made in the USA
Monee, IL
16 July 2020

36033325R00125